Rachel And

Learning About
Friendship

by the same author

The Red Beast
Controlling Anger in Children with Asperger's Syndrome
K.I. Al-Ghani
Illustrated by Haitham Al-Ghani
ISBN 978 1 84310 943 3
eISBN 978 1 84642 848 7

Making the Move
A Guide for Schools and Parents on the Transfer of Pupils with Autism Spectrum Disorders (ASDs) from Primary to Secondary School
K.I. Al-Ghani and Lynda Kenward
Illustrated by Haitham Al-Ghani
ISBN 978 1 84310 934 1
eISBN 978 1 84642 935 4

of related interest

Liam Says 'Hi'
Learning to Greet a Friend
Jane Whelen Banks
ISBN 978 1 84310 901 3
eISBN 978 1 84642 873 9

Liam Knows What to do When Kids Act Snitty
Coping when Friends are Tactless
Jane Whelen Banks
ISBN 978 1 84310 902 0
eISBN 978 1 84642 872 2

My Social Stories Book
Edited by Carol Gray and Abbie Leigh White
Illustrated by Sean McAndrew
ISBN 978 1 85302 950 9
eISBN 978 0 85700 166 5

Caring for Myself
A Social Skills Storybook
Christy Gast and Jane Krug
Photographs by Kotoe Laackman
ISBN 978 1 84310 872 6 hardback
ISBN 978 1 84310 887 0 paperback
eISBN 978 1 84642 723 7

K.I. Al-Ghani
Illustrated by Haitham Al-Ghani

Learning About Friendship

Stories to Support Social Skills Training in Children with Asperger Syndrome and High Functioning Autism

Jessica Kingsley *Publishers*
London and Philadelphia

First published in 2011
by Jessica Kingsley Publishers
73 Collier Street
London N1 9BE, UK
and
400 Market Street, Suite 400
Philadelphia, PA 19106, USA

www.jkp.com

Copyright © K.I. Al-Ghani 2011

Illustrations copyright © Haitham Al-Ghani 2011

All rights reserved. No part of this publication may be reproduced in any material form (including photocopying or storing it in any medium by electronic means and whether or not transiently or incidentally to some other use of this publication) without the written permission of the copyright owner except in accordance with the provisions of the Copyright, Designs and Patents Act 1988 or under the terms of a licence issued by the Copyright Licensing Agency Ltd, Saffron House, 6–10 Kirby Street, London EC1N 8TS. Applications for the copyright owner's written permission to reproduce any part of this publication should be addressed to the publisher.

Warning: The doing of an unauthorized act in relation to a copyright work may result in both a civil claim for damages and criminal prosecution.

Library of Congress Cataloging in Publication Data
A CIP catalog record for this book is available from the Library of Congress

British Library Cataloguing in Publication Data
A CIP catalogue record for this book is available from the British Library

ISBN 978 1 84905 145 3
eISBN 978 0 85700 348 5

Printed and bound in Great Britain by Bell and Bain ltd, Glasgow

This book is dedicated to Ahmed and Sarah Al-Ghani
for their love, support and encouragement.

Contents

INTRODUCTION 9

1. The Dinosaurs: A Story About Starting School and Learning to Share — 13
   Overview 13
   Story 15

2. Spit and Chase: A Story About Joining in Playground Games — 23
   Overview 23
   Story 25

3. Golden Hour: A Story About Winning/Losing, Taking Turns and Managing Anger — 33
   Overview 33
   Story 35

4. Timothy Tattletale: A Story About When to Tell — 43
   Overview 43
   Story 45

5. Too Much Thomas the Tank Engine: A Story About Obsessions — 57
   Overview 57
   Story 59

6. Ablutions: A Story About Personal Hygiene — 69
   Overview 69
   Story 71

7. Space Invaders: A Story About Personal Space — 83
   Overview — 83
   Story — 85

8. Billy Blunt: A Story About Using Tact and Diplomacy — 95
   Overview — 95
   Story — 97

9. The Barbie Club: A Story About Being Taken Advantage Of — 107
   Overview — 107
   Story — 108

10. The Beach Ball: A Story About Jealousy and What Makes a Friend — 125
    Overview — 125
    Story — 126

Appendix: Useful Books and Resources — 143

Introduction

Children with Asperger Syndrome (AS) and high functioning autism (HFA), all have difficulties, to a greater or lesser degree, in the following three crucial areas.

1. Social integration – making and maintaining friendships

In children with autistic spectrum disorder (ASD) this can often be seen during play with classmates. These children want to have friends, but they lack the intrinsic social skills needed to make and maintain friendships and, because of this, they spend much less time involved in trying to make friends.

These children may show difficulties with adapting their behaviour to fit in with the group. This is often seen as a difficulty with co-operating, with reciprocity and with assertiveness. They can unwittingly show a complete lack of empathy. This leads to them being avoided by their peers, and so social anxiety and isolation begin to take hold.

Problems with understanding the unwritten rules of social conduct mean they can easily say and do the wrong thing. This can be, at best, amusing, but it can also be embarrassing or offensive. Their honesty and lack of guile means they can be perceived as being either innocent and gullible, or arrogant, impertinent and rude.

Difficulty with body awareness also means they may innocently encroach upon someone else's personal space, making that person feel uncomfortable or threatened.

2. Social communication – understanding language

This includes both verbal and non-verbal communication. The non-verbal aspects will relate to facial expression, body language, gesturing and eye contact. They may find it difficult to have a conversation and to follow non-verbal cues.

Learning About Friendship

Although they usually have no difficulty in talking, they often fail to take into account the needs of the listener. It is easy for them to become boring or pedantic.

The verbal aspects may result in language being taken literally, and so nuance, sarcasm, irony and metaphorical speech can escape the listener with ASD.

3. Social imagination – predicting what others will do and say and understanding the intentions behind people's actions

This relates to a deficit in the development of what is known as a 'Theory of Mind' (ToM) – that ability to be aware of what other people may think, know, wish or believe and the ability to understand intentions and predict behaviour.

Impairment of social imagination also relates to the child with ASD being involved in repetitive activities and restricted behaviours.

These children often develop intense interests in specific areas like dinosaurs, cars, vacuum cleaners, Doctor Who, Thomas the Tank Engine or Lego, to name just a few. Unlike neurotypical (NT) children, who can also develop hobbies and interests, the interests of the child with ASD are not usually linked to any current social trend or fashion. These interests also usually persist for much longer than

Introduction

they would with an NT child – some adults with ASD continue to enjoy Lego, Star Wars, comic books, Disney cartoons, etc. These consuming interests may also lead to a failure to see that others are not really interested in their hobbies or obsessions. (A lack of *social* imagination should not be confused with a lack of imagination – some children with AS are highly imaginative.)

Current best practice advocates teaching social skills in a direct and explicit way. Whilst there are many excellent social-skills training programmes to choose from (see the Appendix to this book), there are very few stories that have been written especially for children with ASD in order to address these social skills.

This book therefore contains stories that target typical problem areas I encounter in my work as a specialist teacher for inclusion support. I have found that advising teachers to use a story format helps to depersonalize the issues and allows the children to see things from the perspective of others.

Children with ASD respond well to visual stories as they are usually hypersensitive to perceived criticism and tackling a social issue head on can often be met with a refusal to acknowledge a problem or total disengagement. Using the story helps the child to stand outside the situation and look on. They have often then been able to recognize themselves in the story, and this opens the door to discussion – which, in turn, leads to useful insight and strategies they can practise and implement in the future.

The stories in this book could form the opening to any social-skills training lesson, whether at home or at school. They target key problem areas such as: sharing; taking turns; being a tattletale; obsessions; winning and losing; being taken advantage of; jealousy; personal space; personal hygiene; and defining friendship. Unlike other stories, they do not assume that the child has innate social skills. In this way, not only will the child with ASD gain useful insight, but siblings and peers can also be helped to understand the nature of ASD and how it affects social cognition.

If these social deficits are so crucial, we may well ask how we can hope to help the child with AS or HFA make and keep friends. Many of the skills needed to make friends are so intuitive that we never have to teach them. Most social-skills programmes simply assume that children already have these abilities and are therefore not very helpful for the child struggling with ASD. It is, therefore, important to use programmes specially designed for the child with ASD. We may also question, if the deficits are so great, what the child/adult with ASD can bring to a friendship – why would anyone *want* to befriend them? What we should keep in mind here is the fact that these children, and later adults, bring with them a unique and quaint perspective of the world. Given a chance, they can make a superb friend, husband/wife, father/mother.

Let's just look at what they can bring to the NT world:

- Children and adults with ASD are honest; they seldom tell lies (and even if they do, they are not very good at it!).

- They are loyal and true, non-judgemental, not usually materialistic and never knowingly unkind.

- They are not sarcastic or vindictive; can be endearingly innocent; stick to the rules, and have a keen sense of justice and equity.

- What you see is what you get: no duplicity, backbiting or gossiping.

All of these qualities are of great value, and by helping those children, and later adults, to find their way in the social world, we can ensure that others will see that they have a positive contribution to make.

Story 1

The Dinosaurs

A Story About Starting School and Learning to Share

Overview

Quite often, children with ASD, are totally egocentric. At a young age they are single-minded about getting what they want and often fail to understand when other people come in between them and their goal. This story illustrates a typical problem – sharing and having an awareness of the needs of others.

In this story the child, George, has been encouraged to look forward to school with the promise that there will be favourite toys to play with. A Social Story™ (a technique devised by Carol Gray – see Appendix for details) has been written to make the transition to school less stressful for George. However, he becomes increasingly anxious to go to school and repeats the same question: "Is it school today?" His mother has to show passage of time by using a calendar and crossing off the days, which is an excellent way to get children with ASD to anticipate a happy event.

Once at school, the boy heads straight for the dinosaurs, ignoring another child sitting there. He has been told that he can play with the dinosaurs and is not being deliberately unkind to the other child – he just has not seen the child, only the dinosaurs. This sort of misunderstanding happens frequently in classrooms.

By introducing the story and then role-playing the scenario, it is possible to teach the child the rules about sharing. Learning this rule can be a valuable tool when it comes to building friendships. During the role-play, the child should be

Learning About Friendship

encouraged to act the parts of all the characters in the story. This will enable him to see what has happened from the perspective of another person:

- What did the teacher think when she saw him take the toys?
- What did his mum think?
- What did the boy think?

All these questions would never spontaneously enter his head. A child with ASD would only be able to see events from his own perspective. The scenario will need to be practised many times before the child will be able to use this skill spontaneously, and then you will still need to be careful that they do not apply it only to dinosaurs!! Parents, siblings, teachers and classmates are sometimes unwittingly guilty of condoning behaviour that will later lead to social difficulties.

Let us take the example of sharing. At home, the child with ASD will have become quite upset at the thought of sharing possessions with siblings and so both parents and siblings have learned to not push this issue. However, almost as soon as the child starts school this problem will manifest itself. By making allowances for the child and allowing him to be selfish, we make it more difficult for that child to make friends. In such situations one can use the story as an opening strategy and then give the child many opportunities to practise sharing and taking turns under adult supervision. Remember always to praise and reward instances of sharing.

The Dinosaurs

George was going to start school in September. George's mum had told him there would be lots of toys and children to play with.

She had a special book with photographs all about his new school. It had a picture of George's classroom, his teacher and his classmates.

Learning About Friendship

"Will they have dinosaurs in school?" asked George, hopefully. George just loved dinosaurs. He had a huge collection in his bedroom. They took pride of place on his cupboard, where he loved nothing better than to line them up and reel off their long names to himself and to anyone who would listen.

"Can I play with the dinosaurs in school?" George asked, earnestly.

"Yes, of course you can," said Mum, encouragingly.

George just could not get the idea of school and dinosaurs out of his mind.

He asked Mum every morning, "Is it school today?"

Mum had to get a calendar and show George how to cross off the days until it was time for school.

The Dinosaurs

Learning About Friendship

Finally, the big day came and George raced ahead of Mum all the way to school.

"Hey, wait for me, George," shouted Mum. But George did not hear her. His head was filled with dinosaurs!

George raced into school and found his classroom. He could remember the door from the storybook Mum had shown him. Pushing it open George hurried inside. He did not see or hear the teacher as she said "Good morning". He did not notice the other children. His eyes went straight over to the corner of the room and there they were – the dinosaurs. George was so excited.

He raced up to the dinosaurs and scooped them all up in his arms. He wanted to start lining them up in order of size, since they were strewn rather untidily across the floor.

Suddenly there was an ear-piercing scream. George had not noticed the little boy already playing with the dinosaurs.

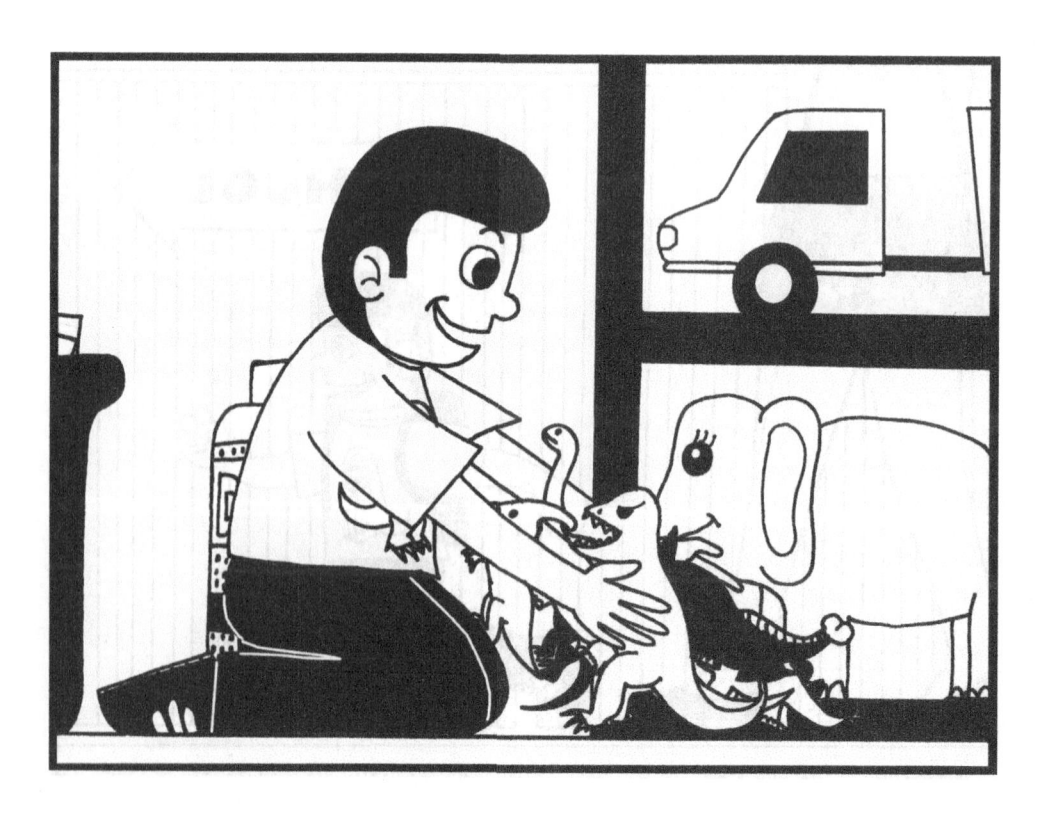

The Dinosaurs

The next thing George knew was that Mum was very cross and the teacher was very cross. They took away the dinosaurs and gave them to the screaming boy.

George became very upset and confused. He had been waiting to play with the dinosaurs for weeks.

Mum and the teacher took George out of the classroom and into the next room. Mum cuddled George until he began to calm down and between his sobs she explained that another boy had been playing with the dinosaurs. When George grabbed all the dinosaurs this had made that boy very upset. The teacher had taken the dinosaurs away because she thought George was being unkind.

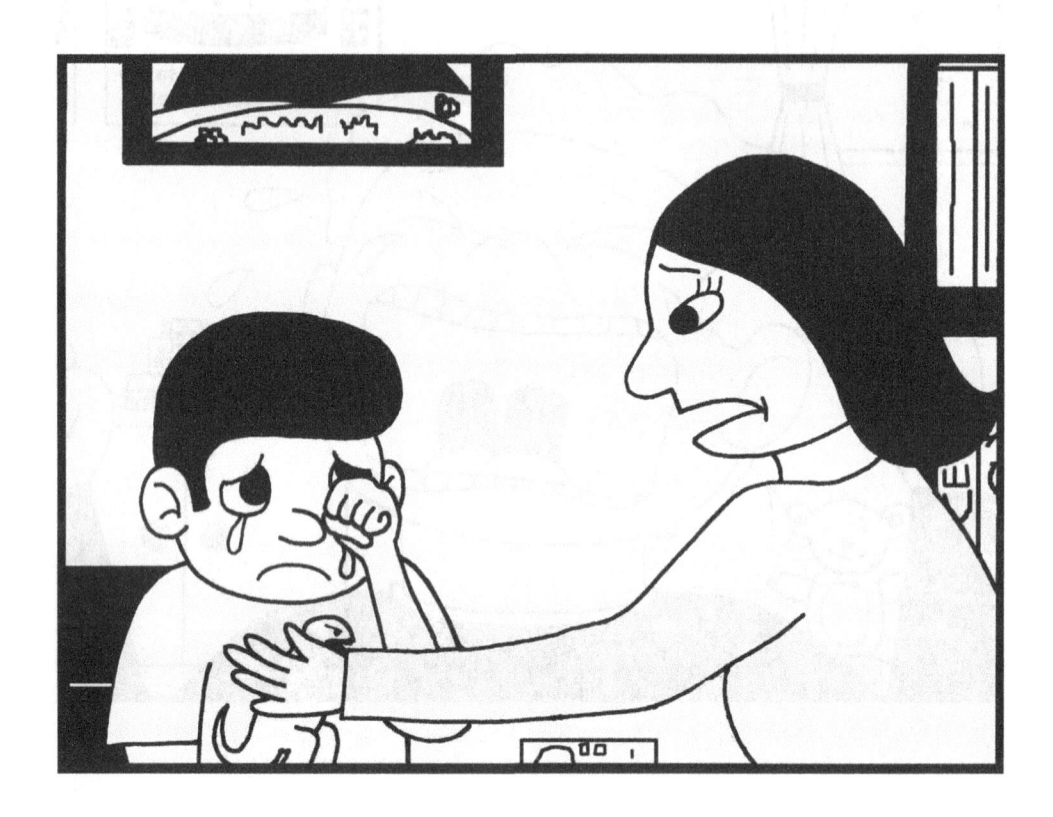

The Dinosaurs

Mum took George back into the classroom and, holding his hand, they went up to the boy playing with the dinosaurs.

Mum showed George how he could ask to share the dinosaurs, and suddenly George had hold of a T-Rex. This was his favourite dinosaur!

Learning About Friendship

Mum and the teacher made a special book all about the dinosaurs. In the book they explained about having to share things in the classroom.

George would try to remember to ask and share if someone was already playing with the dinosaurs.

When the teacher saw George playing nicely she gave him a lovely dinosaur sticker to put on his T-shirt.

Guess what? It was a T-Rex sticker!

Story 2

Spit and Chase

A Story About Joining in Playground Games

Overview

This story is based on a real-life scenario.

The school playground can be a confusing place for a child with ASD. They love the freedom to run and jump about with other children, but fail to notice the overtures of friendship that are happening, or the invention of spontaneous games with instant rule changes.

Children with ASD will often use inappropriate strategies when trying to get the attention of adults and children alike. Spitting is one of the more unpleasant ones and causes great concern for both teachers and parents. How do you get the child with ASD to see that it is a huge social no-no? If you mention the behaviour you run the risk of reinforcing it. The child quickly learns it will get them noticed and so they use it again and, before you know it, it becomes a little ritual and part of the child's daily repertoire. The key is to ignore the behaviour, but not the *need*.

In this story a young girl, Susie, is spitting at her classmates in the playground. The teacher is, quite rightly, distressed and she tells the girl she must let her mother know about the incident. What the teacher has failed to realize is that the little girl is unperturbed; in fact, she takes this as a compliment!

In the real-life story, the girl's mother could not imagine where her daughter had learned this rather unsavoury habit – it certainly was not at home. However, after a little detective work, we found out that she had, indeed, learned it at home – from the cat! The cat had spat at the dog, which, incensed, had chased it out of the garden. All the little girl wanted was to be chased. This was the 'need' behind the behaviour. She did not have the social tools to ask for this – so she invented a rather successful methodology. She felt sure everyone would see how clever she was. Mystery over, it was relatively easy to remedy.

Incidents like this happen all the time. Some children push or hit out when they want attention; they may snatch the ball being used for a game of football. They do not see that this is inappropriate – after all, to them, the children are just running about kicking a ball and they would like to join in. They do not understand the rules of the game, they cannot read the body language of the annoyed children or understand their protestations. It is only when someone rudely snatches the ball back and then marches them indoors, that they become aware something is wrong. However, in their own head they were not doing anything wrong. Time for a meltdown! (Notice in the story how the teacher used a 'Happy Scrap Book' as a means to calm the child, before tackling the issue.)

Spit and Chase

Susie usually enjoyed recess. However, these days her classmates did not seem interested in playing 'chase', Susie's favourite game. They were all involved in the latest pastime – skipping. Susie hated skipping and all the children wanted to do was skip. Susie tried running up and down the playground on her own, but it wasn't as much fun as being chased!

Learning About Friendship

Earlier that morning, Susie had seen Cookie, the neighbour's cat, spit at their dog, Arnold. Arnold had become angry and barked loudly. He had chased Cookie out of the garden. Susie had an idea.

Spit and Chase

At lunchtime recess, as the children were skipping, Susie went up to Joan, who was turning the rope.

"Hi, Susie," smiled Joan, "do you want to join in?"

Susie did not say anything, but as Joan turned to watch the children skipping, Susie spat at her.

Learning About Friendship

Joan was shocked and very angry. She threw down the rope and chased Susie all over the playground.

"You disgusting thing!" shouted Joan.

Susie could not hear Joan. She did not see how angry and upset Joan was. Susie was enjoying being chased all around the playground – she thought it was great fun. She was sure Joan must have been enjoying it too!

Spit and Chase

After playtime, Mrs Coulson, the class teacher, called Susie to her desk. "Susie, Joan said you spat at her today. Is this true?" enquired Mrs Coulson, earnestly.

"Yes, Mrs Coulson," answered Susie, truthfully.

"Well, I am going to have to tell your mother about this," said Mrs Coulson, sternly.

Susie heard the words Mrs Coulson had said, but she did not notice that Mrs Coulson seemed angry. Susie felt very pleased with herself. Now Mummy would see how clever she was.

Learning About Friendship

During afternoon playtime Susie spat again. This time at Timmy Jones. Timmy was furious.

"You dirty little girl!" he yelled as he began to chase Susie around the playground.

Mrs Coulson had witnessed the incident and she ran over to Susie. Taking her by the hand she led Susie back into school.

"No more playtime for you, Susie," said Mrs Coulson, sharply.

Spit and Chase

Susie was very confused. Recess had only just begun and she was having a lovely time being chased by Timmy.

Why was Mrs Coulson so angry?

The teacher took Susie to the quiet room. She gave Susie her 'Happy Scrap Book' to look at. This was a book filled with pictures of things that Susie loved: her mum and dad, Arnold the dog, Susie's collection of Beanie Babies, her dad's aquarium, chocolate cake, the swimming pool and many, many, more interesting pictures. Looking at the book made Susie calm down. She stopped crying and Mrs Coulson gave her a glass of water and a handful of raisins.

Learning About Friendship

"Susie, why did you spit at Timmy just now?" asked Mrs Coulson, calmly.

"I wanted him to chase me," answered Susie, "like Arnold chased Cookie the cat."

"Oh, I see," said the teacher, kindly. "I will give you a special card to show the children if you want to play chase."

Mrs Coulson explained that spitting was only for angry cats and bad-tempered camels – not friendly little girls like Susie.

Next day at recess Susie showed Timmy Jones the special 'chase me' card. Luckily, Timmy hated skipping too, so he had a fun time playing chase with Susie until it was time to go back into class.

From then on, Susie always remembered that spitting was just for angry cats and bad-tempered camels!

Story 3

Golden Hour

A Story About Winning/Losing, Taking Turns and Managing Anger

Overview

I cannot begin to count the number of times the issue of poor sportsmanship turns up when dealing with children with ASD. These children and games of chance do not really seem to go hand in hand. Yet, they are a very effective tool in teaching turn-taking, patience and anticipation. Some children with ASD just accept their limitations and shun board games with a vengeance – but, often, by implementing a few strategies it is possible to make these an enjoyable experience for them.

Planning ahead is the key. The child will need to know what the game entails and that there will be winners and losers. A social story, winner/loser cue card and reward system is all that is needed to turn this sort of activity around and make it fun for all involved.

In this story we see a number of issues emerging in relation to James, the child with ASD. First, there is the overture of friendship towards him given by Judy. Judy is not too concerned about what they play, but she would like to play with James and invites him for a game of Snakes & Ladders. James would much rather be doing Lego, but since the teacher had asked them to try something new, he reluctantly agrees to one game. (He did not think to ask Judy to join him for Lego – he could not read her intentions and was unaware that she wanted to be friendly.) You will note the way he rather rudely snatches the red counter. Judy is used to this sort of behaviour from James and gives in to his demands.

However, after reading the story, discuss this point with the child, and ask him if he can see how people would think this rude and inconsiderate. If he *cannot* see it, then role-play the incident, letting the child play the part of Judy.

You take on the role of James and ask him to see how he feels when you snatch his counter away. This may take practice; children with ASD are not natural role-players since this takes a degree of pretend play, which they find difficult. However, once they get the hang of it they can do it well – and, indeed, many then like to take this further and go on to do Amateur Dramatics.

The next problem is that of taking turns and probability. Judy gently coaches James through this, but it is not long before he loses control and goes into an almighty tantrum.

Children with ASD yearn to have control. They prefer non-competitive games and games in which they can predict the outcome. It takes a large amount of emotional maturity to be a good sport. Most children achieve this by the age of eight or nine years. For a child with ASD we should always think in terms of them being a couple of years out of step with NT children. However, it is never too early to start the training.

Keep a supply of 'good sport' stickers and use these to enable the child to work towards a reward of his choice. He or she may not appreciate or really enjoy the fun elements of board games, but they can practise being a good sport. Show the child that while he may 'lose' the game, he can always 'win' the friendship game.

The story also deals with the issue of anger management. In it, the teacher has a strategy to help James to calm himself in the situation, and later they can address the problem he had with Judy and look for solutions.

Golden Hour

It was Friday afternoon and 'Golden Hour'. During the last hour of school each Friday, the teacher let the children choose a favourite activity if they had worked hard all week.

James loved 'Golden Hour'. He usually played with Lego bricks by himself, but today Mrs Linfield had asked everyone to try something new.

Learning About Friendship

Judy Lopez liked James; he was handsome and funny. However, James always seemed to enjoy playing on his own. This was her chance to ask him if he would play with her.

"James, please play Snakes & Ladders with me," she asked James, shyly.

James was a little annoyed. 'Golden Hour' was supposed to be free choice and he really wanted to play with the Lego. However, he remembered Mrs Linfield's request and so he reluctantly agreed.

"Oh, okay," said James, petulantly, "but just *one* game!" he stressed.

Golden Hour

Judy felt really excited. She took the box of Snakes & Ladders off the shelf and set it down on the floor. After removing the board, she chose a red counter and picked up the dice.

"Hey, I want red!" shouted James, rudely. "It's my favourite colour."

Judy handed the red counter to him. James could be very determined and she really wanted to play with him.

"First person to throw a six moves first," said Judy.

James snatched the dice from Judy's hand and threw it, but it landed on a two.

Learning About Friendship

James picked up the dice to throw again.

"It's my turn now," Judy reminded James, kindly.

"But I have to get a six or else I can't move," grumbled James.

"No, it's the *first person* who throws a six who gets to move first, then the other person can throw and move," explained Judy, patiently.

Judy threw the dice and it was a three. James was so relieved, now he could get a six. He threw again, but this time it was only a one.

"My turn," said Judy, cheerfully.

To Judy's delight, she threw a six. James felt cross.

"That was my six. If I had thrown again it would have been me," thought James, unreasonably.

As the game continued, James became more and more excited. He went up two ladders, but then had to go down a very long snake. Judy was ahead of him. If she threw a five she would be the winner. Judy blew on the dice and out rolled a five.

James' anger bubbled up inside of him. He grabbed the board and tossed it in the air, in a fit of temper.

"CHEAT! CHEAT! You're a CHEAT!" screamed James, accusingly.

Judy's face crumpled.

Learning About Friendship

"I'm not a cheat, I'm not," she pleaded.

Then, covering her face with her hands, she began to sob loudly.

By this time, Mrs Linfield was on the scene.

"Take five minutes' 'Time Out', immediately," she told James, sternly, handing him the sand-timer.

Mrs Linfield turned to soothe poor Judy.

"It's all right, Judy, don't cry," she said, consolingly. "You know James hates to lose and he has a problem understanding board games."

Golden Hour

James took the five-minute timer and went to the 'Time Out' corner. He had practised this with Mrs Linfield and he knew what to do. Taking deep breaths he watched the grains of sand as they fell. After five minutes James had calmed down. Mrs Linfield called him and Judy to the book corner to speak to them.

"Now, James, could we have done something better to avoid this upset?" asked Mrs Linfield, searchingly.

James felt ashamed; he knew he shouldn't have thrown the board or called Judy a cheat, but he just couldn't control his bad temper.

"Well, I didn't want to play Snakes & Ladders – I wanted Lego, but Judy asked and I didn't want to be unfriendly," he tried to explain.

"What could you have done then?" Mrs Linfield asked.

"I guess I should have asked Judy to do Lego with me instead," said James, wisely.

"That would have been a great idea," enthused the teacher.

Learning About Friendship

"Judy likes you and she wanted to be your friend. I am sure she would have been happy doing Lego with you," she continued.

"Oh, yes, I would love to do Lego with James," Judy whispered, her eyes sparkling.

"Off you go and play Lego," instructed Mrs Linfield. "And remember, James, kind words and kind actions are the sure way to make friends."

Judy and James went to get the Lego box.

"I'm sorry, Judy," said James, sheepishly, as he opened the box. "Shall we build a red house?" he asked Judy, kindly.

"Oh, yes please," sighed Judy with a smile.

Story 4

Timothy Tattletale

A Story About When to Tell

Overview

I think most class teachers will say they have a Timothy Tattletale in their class, irrespective of autism. Children who appoint themselves as class informer usually do it to gain the attention and approval of the teacher, and they can do it overtly or surreptitiously. They are usually aware of the impact it has on the children, but because they are generally unpopular, the role gets them negative attention – which is often seen as preferable to getting no attention at all!

Children with ASD become the class tell tale for somewhat different reasons. They cannot conceive of the notion that children will openly flout the rules, knowingly. Their 'black and white' thinking leaves no room for this possibility and so they often feel they are being helpful by pointing out the rule break. In fact, these children can find themselves in trouble for rule breaking almost every day in the early years of school life. It is only as they become aware of classroom and school rules that they learn to do something about it. Quite often it is a relief. They need to know so many things, which many of us know through 'common sense'. These children have a woeful lack of 'common sense' and are judged accordingly.

In this story we see that Timothy has been empowered by the knowledge of rules, especially written rules! He has at last learned how to gain positive attention and the approval of the important adults in his life. He is anxious to share his new-found knowledge with his classmates; however, he does not realize the impact this will have on his ability to make and maintain friends.

We see that a smart teacher has prepared Timothy well for his transition to a new class. He is aware of Timothy's need to be told explicitly what behaviour is expected of him. In the story, the use of an individual workstation and transition book*, all help to reduce Timothy's anxiety. However, after just one morning in his new class, Timothy unwittingly manages to alienate his classmates and set off alarm bells with his well-meaning teacher.

It is interesting to see that Timothy is unable to comprehend the non-verbal signals sent by the children. Bobby's conspiratorial wink is completely lost on Timothy, as is Carol's warm smile. This is an area that will need much development if social skills are to improve. Role-play and analysing TV programmes can help to develop these skills.

The playground is often a dangerous area for children with ASD. Poor social skills can lead to them becoming the victims of bullying. It is therefore essential that these children be adequately supervised when on the school playground.

Another area of difficulty for these children is deception. Timothy was very confused when Bobby turned from bully to best mate as soon as a teacher was on the scene.

It is interesting to see that Timothy had not factored in the feelings of his classmates when he chose to expose their rule-breaking to the teacher. This inability to predict the behaviour of others is all part of the deficit in social imagination, shared by all children on the Autism Spectrum. It is important that children like Timothy know when it is acceptable to 'tell'. Their natural naivety can make them a victim for the more unscrupulous child.

The model of 'think and then decide' is an important one to practise with these children to help them to be less impulsive. Inventing and role-playing case-specific scenarios can help the child to build up a repertoire of when to tell and when to stay silent.

One area (not covered in the story), is that of rule-breaking during games and PE. It is often a good idea to train children with ASD as referees because they can then use their ability to spot rule-breakers legitimately, and they will learn that it is okay to point out rule infringements if you are in charge. However, it may still cost them friendships!

Be careful to question these children to ensure they understand words like 'discreet'. This concept may need to be practised frequently before they truly understand it. Their lack of social imagination means that children with ASD are often very unselfconscious – something that inevitably alienates them from their NT classmates, who will become increasingly self-conscious as they approach their teenage years.

---

* A transition book would contain all the information the child may need about the new class.

Timothy Tattletale

After the summer vacation, Timothy would be moving up to a new class. Up to now school life had been very confusing for him; he seemed to get into trouble all of the time. However, since he had learned to read the school rules he was beginning to enjoy himself more.

Timothy was a stickler for the rules. You knew where you stood with rules. He loved to see them written down in long lists. He had made up his mind to do his very best to follow all of the school rules this year. That way the teachers would be happy, Mummy and Daddy would be happy and he would earn lots of rewards! Timothy could not wait to get back to school.

Learning About Friendship

At last, the first day of the new school year arrived. Timothy was going to be in Mr Truman's class. He knew all about the class because Mr Truman had made him a special book. It had photographs of the room, his workstation, the class assistants and all the children. Yes, sir! Timothy was more than ready. He knew that Mr Truman was strict, but fair, and he had a list of the class rules to follow. Timothy felt he was going to enjoy this school year.

Timothy Tattletale

The first lesson of the day was 'Penmanship'. Timothy was not very good at handwriting, but one of the rules was: 'DO YOUR BEST'. He decided he would try extra hard to form the letters neatly.

Seated across from him was Bobby Jenkins. Bobby hated 'Penmanship' too. He turned to Timothy and winked at him. It was then that Timothy spotted Bobby putting today's date on a page of handwriting that he had completed last school year in Mrs Brown's class. Timothy felt indignant: that had to be against the rules. Timothy's hand shot up. (He remembered the rule about raising your hand and not calling out.)

"Yes, Timothy," enquired Mr Truman, as he looked up from the register.

"Please sir, Bobby Jenkins isn't doing his 'Penmanship' exercise, he has put the date on work he has already done," blurted out Timothy, accusingly.

Learning About Friendship

"Thank you, Timothy," said Mr Truman. "Bobby, bring your book out here. Thank you," instructed Mr Truman, quietly.

Timothy noticed Mr Truman never said 'please' – he always ended an instruction with 'thank you': this way the student did not have a choice. Mr Truman expected you to do what he asked, without question.

Bobby stared at Timothy; he could not believe Timothy had just told on him! As he passed Timothy's desk he glared at him. "You rotten little tattler! I'll get you for this," spat out Bobby under his breath.

Timothy carried on with his handwriting. "You were breaking the rules," he answered, calmly.

Timothy Tattletale

The rest of the morning passed without incident, but just as the class were lining up to go out for recess, Timothy noticed Carol Fletcher pop a stick of chewing gum in her mouth. Carol looked across at Timothy and smiled. Timothy liked Carol; she was always friendly towards him. He could not let her get into trouble for breaking the rules.

Timothy put his hand up.

"Yes, Timothy?" said Mr Truman.

"Carol Fletcher is chewing gum," chanted Timothy.

Mr Truman looked up from his desk.

"Carol," he said, with a sigh.

Carol, she felt quite upset. She had always been kind to Timothy and now he had just told. He was turning into such a tattletale. There was something about that boy, she thought as she threw her newly chewed gum into the bin.

Out in the playground, Bobby rushed up to Timothy.

"What is wrong with you? You idiot," he challenged Timothy. "Why did you tell on Carol and me?"

"You both broke the rules," Timothy answered, truthfully.

"Oh, yeah! Who died and made you the rule detective?" asked Bobby, sarcastically.

By now a group of children had gathered around the two boys. Sensing an argument brewing, they were eager to see what would happen next. However, Mrs Brackpool, the Special Ed. teacher, was on playground duty that morning and she quickly dispersed the crowd.

"Everything all right here, boys?" she asked Bobby.

"Er, yes, Miss," answered Bobby, slyly, as he put his arm around Timothy's shoulder. "Everything is just fine."

As soon as they were out of earshot of Mrs Brackpool, Bobby turned to Timothy menacingly.

Timothy Tattletale

"You were lucky that time, Timothy Tattletale, but just tell on me again and see what will happen!" Bobby said, threateningly.

Timothy was confused. Bobby seemed to be angry, but he had put an arm around his shoulder in a friendly way and told Mrs Brackpool that everything was fine. Before he could ponder this further, the bell sounded for end of recess and the class lined up to go back into school.

At the end of the school day, Mr Truman asked Timothy to wait behind so he could speak to him. Timothy felt proud; he was sure Mr Truman was going to thank him for telling on those kids who broke the rules.

"Sit down, Timothy," said Mr Truman, kindly.

"I could not help noticing you let me know about rule-breakers today."

Timothy smiled, "I sure did," he beamed.

"Timothy, how do you think Bobby and Carol felt when you told on them?" asked Mr Truman, raising his eyebrows.

Learning About Friendship

Timothy had not really considered this; he was just following the rules.

"I don't know," he answered, slowly. "Bobby seemed a bit mad at first, but then he put his arm around my shoulder in the playground and told me to tell on him again, and Carol didn't say anything."

"Well, Timothy, let me give you some advice. It is very good that you want to follow the rules. However, you won't make any friends this school year if you keep telling me about children who are breaking the rules. You will make the children feel either very angry or very upset. I know you are anxious that everyone follows the rules, but it really isn't your job," explained Mr Truman, kindly, "and there is a big difference between tattling and telling."

"I think we need to have some new rules about when to tell and when to keep quiet," said Mr Truman with a wink.

Timothy Tattletale

"First, you need to stop and think," continued the teacher. "Sometimes it is okay to tell; for example, if you think the situation is dangerous. If you saw a child smoking in the school building, that could cause a fire; so it would be okay to tell a grown up. If you knew someone was playing truant to see a person they had met on an Internet chat line, they could be in real danger, so it would be the right thing to tell someone. Similarly, if you thought a situation was unkind or hurtful. For example, if someone was name-calling or bullying another child or you caught them stealing something, then it would be okay to tell a grown up. In these cases, you should tell the teacher or another responsible adult, but in a discreet way – don't call out in front of the class unless it is a real emergency," explained Mr Truman, clearly.

Learning About Friendship

Mr Truman stopped and smiled at Timothy.

"I am afraid you are going to see a lot of children breaking the rules. If it is not dangerous or hurtful, it's better to leave the rule-breakers to whoever is in charge," continued Mr Truman with a grin.

"But they might not see them," interrupted Timothy.

"I know, Timothy, but it is not your job to worry about this. Usually rule-breakers will get found out, sooner or later. I think I would have noticed Bobby had not done his handwriting, when I came to mark the books. As for Carol, I am sure the person in charge of the playground would have noticed her chewing." answered Mr Truman, wisely.

Timothy had a lot to think about. Mr Truman made a special sign for him to post in his workstation.

Here is what it said:

WHEN TO TELL:
Think and then decide
Hurtful or dangerous? Then it's okay,
tell a grown up right away.
Other rule-breakers may be at large,
better leave them to whoever's in charge.

Timothy had a brilliant year in Mr Truman's class. He said sorry to Bobby and Carol, explaining that he did not realize the difference between tattling and telling. They forgave him and became firm friends.

Sometimes Timothy was tempted to tell on the rule-breakers, but he went to read his sign first and then usually made the right decision. Mr Truman was so impressed he made Timothy 'Student of the Year'.

Timothy is still a stickler for the rules, but now he knows when to tell and when to keep quiet.

Timothy Tattletale

Story 5

Too Much Thomas the Tank Engine

A Story About Obsessions

Overview

The subject of special interests is one that permeates all layers of the Autism Spectrum. Most parents will be unconcerned, in the early years, when children develop an intense interest in a favourite subject – be it dinosaurs, cars, animals, insects, books or TV characters, to name just a few. However, this intense interest can develop into an all-consuming passion or obsession.

We know from speaking to many individuals with AS or HFA that these interests are developed as a means of bringing moments of tranquillity and happiness into an otherwise frantic and confusing world.

As children grow, however, the innocent obsession with something like Lego can soon become an area of ridicule that can interfere with the development of friendships. The person with ASD is at a loss to understand why others don't find their particular area of expertise equally as fascinating and why people will try to discourage it. As NT children grow up, they have an innate ability to change their pastimes to something more suited to their age. It simply is 'not cool' to be playing with dolls or reading comic books as you get older and become more self-conscious and in need of peer approval.

When children with ASD are younger they become experts in getting what they want. Almost every trip to the shops will result in a new acquisition to add to a growing collection. In the interest of sanity and tranquillity, we parents often use these special interests as a tool to manage behaviour. This, in itself, is a good thing, but a line must be drawn between a harmless 'enthusiasm' and an obsessive self-absorption that blocks out the world.

In this story, we see a typical scenario played out. Harry is enchanted by all things connected to 'Thomas the Tank Engine'. His parents are thrilled with Harry's ability to talk about his hobby. Parents of children with ASD will have been concerned about the development of expressive and receptive language in their child (which is not as evident in children with AS). A special interest may have been just the key needed to unlock the delay seen in the acquisition of speech and language. However, this intense special interest can sometimes block out or prevent other important learning.

In the story, Harry's mind is so consumed with thoughts of Thomas, trains and buses that he cannot access the school curriculum. The teacher is at a loss to know what to do until she comes up with an idea about a 'special box'.

In my work in a school for children with special needs I have seen this strategy work exceedingly well. One boy, who was referred to me because he had reached the final year of Primary (Elementary) School and was still illiterate, is a perfect example. His special interest was Sherlock Holmes, and because he was always 'reading' these books, his teachers (and parents) made the assumption that he could read. However, testing revealed that not only was he illiterate, he did not even know the letters of the alphabet! I invited the parents and the child to attend a weekly literacy lesson with me, followed by an intense home programme. Within six months he was reading fluently. However, in the classroom his teacher was frustrated by his continuing obsession with Sherlock, which made it difficult for him to complete work tasks. She wrote a social story about locking up his thoughts and it worked like a dream. The same strategy has been used successfully with many other children.

I can't promise this will work for every child, but reading this story with your child will give them useful insight into the feelings of others. It is interesting to notice in the story that Harry could not judge why the children were laughing whenever he mentioned his passion. He thought they were thinking the same way as him. Pointing out to a child with ASD that they may, inadvertently, be becoming the class clown, can be a light-bulb moment.

Too Much Thomas the Tank Engine

It all started one Christmas. Harry opened what promised to be another dull and uninteresting present, to find a copy of a book entitled 'Thomas the Tank Engine' by the Rev. W. Awdry. Harry's eyes grew large as he turned the pages and he urged his mummy to read it over and over again.

Learning About Friendship

This was the spark that lit up Harry's interest in all things to do with trains. They became his great passion. At every shopping trip Harry managed to persuade his mummy to add to his growing collection of Thomas books and toys. On getting a book featuring Bertie the Bus, Harry added buses to his 'enthusiasms' (as Granny called them), and by the time Harry started school he knew everything there was to know about Thomas the Tank Engine and his friends.

Too Much Thomas the Tank Engine

At home, Mummy, Daddy, Granny and Granddad encouraged his hobby and they never tired of hearing him talk with confidence and charm about his special interest. However, at school it was becoming a bit of a problem. Harry couldn't seem to concentrate on anything the teacher said. If he heard the words 'Thomas', 'train' or 'bus' he would interrupt the teacher or another child and talk endlessly about his hobby. Miss Blake, his class teacher, was becoming more than a little concerned.

Learning About Friendship

Each Monday morning, Miss Blake would ask the children to be seated on the floor around her chair so she could call the register, take lunch orders and go through the daily timetable.

"John Adams," called out the teacher.

"Here, Miss Blake," answered John.

"Denise Brown," she chanted as she ticked off the names.

"Here, Miss Blake," came the reply.

"Thomas Cooper," she continued.

"Thomas got stuck in the snow and had to be pulled out," interrupted Harry.

All the children laughed. Harry thought they were laughing at the plight of Thomas the Tank Engine. He carried on talking about the story and did not seem to notice how cross Miss Blake was becoming until Celia, his helper, told him to stand up and follow her. Still talking non-stop about Thomas and the snow, Harry was taken out of the classroom. All the children looked at each other and laughed out loud until Miss Blake instructed them to "Be quiet!"

Almost every day at registration Harry would interrupt. Miss Blake tried everything she could to remind Harry to sit quietly and listen for his name, but he just could not stop himself. Miss Blake arranged for Harry to work with Celia during registration, but now he was finding it difficult to do *any* schoolwork. When he was given a maths or literacy task he would find himself daydreaming about Thomas and his friends.

A special meeting was called with Harry's parents and they all agreed something needed to be done. Harry's father threatened to take all of Harry's collection away unless he got on with his schoolwork. Harry tried very hard, but he just could not stop the thoughts buzzing around in his head.

Learning About Friendship

Then Miss Blake had an idea. She got a special box with a little padlock and key. If Harry's thoughts were becoming a problem they needed to be locked up during work times! The teacher sat down to write a special story for Harry all about the box. Here is what it said:

> The Thought Box
>
> Harry loves Thomas the Tank Engine and all his Friends. Harry's head is filled with thoughts about Thomas, trains and buses.
> At school, all the children learn how to do new skills like reading and maths.
> The children need to think carefully about these new skills.
> Harry's thoughts about Thomas are stopping him from putting the new skills in his head.
> Miss Blake has a special box with a padlock and key.
> Each morning Harry will put all his thoughts about Thomas into the box and Miss Blake will lock them in.
> Harry can have the key to open the box at playtime, lunch time and choosing time.
> Harry will try to keep his thoughts about Thomas in the box when he is doing his schoolwork.
> Miss Blake, Mummy, Daddy, Granny and Granddad will be very happy when they see Harry can do his schoolwork.
> Learning new skills like reading, means Harry can read books by himself.
> Learning new skills is a smart thing to do.

Miss Blake gave a copy of the story to Harry's parents and they read it to him that night before he fell asleep.

On Monday morning, Harry and Miss Blake put all the books and toys about Thomas the Tank Engine into the box and Harry tried hard to imagine his thoughts going into the box with them.

Too Much Thomas the Tank Engine

"Are they all in there, Harry?" the teacher asked with a wink.

"I think so," said Harry, thoughtfully.

"Right, quick, lock the box!" shouted Miss Blake.

Harry laughed out loud. It was funny to think of locking up his thoughts as if they were prisoners!

Miss Blake put the key on a ribbon around her neck.

Learning About Friendship

The first task of that day was number work. Thomas knew all his numbers to one hundred and Miss Blake asked him to put some numbers in a line starting with the smallest. Harry thought he would line them up just like a train; he was about to talk about Thomas when Miss Blake showed him the key. "Oh, yes," thought Harry, "look at the numbers, put them in order starting with the smallest."

In no time at all Harry had completed the task. Miss Blake was so pleased that she smiled brightly and gave Harry a token to put in the class jar. When this jar was full, all the class were going to have pizza! Harry felt very proud as he put his token in the jar and saw the admiring glances of his classmates and Celia.

Too Much Thomas the Tank Engine

Harry worked very hard that day and Miss Blake said he had done more work in that one day than he had done since the beginning of the term. Harry's family were thrilled with the news, and as a special celebration they watched an episode of *Thomas the Tank Engine* on television and Harry's mum made pizza for tea.

These days Harry still loves Thomas and his friends, but he has learned how to lock up his thoughts to give his brain a chance to do new things. He can still talk endlessly about his 'enthusiasm' but he has learned to ask people if they would like to hear more before continuing. Harry's best friend, Verne, shares his passion for Thomas and he is always eager to hear more.

Nowadays, when the register is called, the boy called Thomas has agreed to be called Tommy so Harry can start the day off well. Harry's thoughts of Thomas the Tank Engine are securely locked up in that special box until recess.

Story 6

Ablutions

A Story About Personal Hygiene

Overview

From a very early age, issues surrounding personal hygiene, can have a huge effect on the quality of family life. Many young children with ASD have difficulty with some sensory aspects connected to the need to stay clean. This could be having their hair shampooed or cut; being immersed in a bath or put under a shower; nail cutting; tooth brushing; and general toileting. It is not uncommon for these children to carry these phobias well into adult life, when they can become a constant bone of contention.

When children are younger it is easier for a parent or carer to take control and simply do what is necessary, even if met with opposition. However, as the years pass, this approach becomes increasingly difficult. The use of reward systems can help to ensure that the necessary ablutions are carried out daily; however, what is needed is stoicism on the part of the young person with ASD and a different mind-set. In order for a breakthrough to occur, the young person needs to develop just a little self-awareness and more altruistic feelings towards friends and family. Only then will a personal-hygiene programme become part of an acceptable daily routine.

By taking the young person outside of the situation and letting them see the views of others, it is often possible for them to see the need for personal hygiene. The resultant change in attitude in their nearest and dearest is then sufficient reinforcement for them to continue to persevere. As soon as personal hygiene becomes part of a daily ritual, success is just over the horizon. Positive reactions from classmates may be just the push needed for them to realize that personal hygiene is an essential tool to the development of friendships.

In this story I have deliberately used the word 'ablutions' since it will be unknown to the children. Introducing this story to a child who is sensitive to the words 'washing', 'tooth-brushing', etc., may mean that they refuse to listen. Using the word 'ablutions' may get them past first base and, one hopes, they will be able relate to poor Gordon as his mum urges him to brush his teeth.

When starting this story I usually ask the children if they know the word 'ablutions' and then I set them a challenge, with the promise of a reward, if they can tell me what it means by the end of the story.

Ablutions

"Gordon Norville! I am not going to ask again. Have you brushed your teeth?" shouted Mum as she stood at the foot of the stairs.

"Yes, Mum," Gordon answered, with a sigh. For as long as he could remember, he and his mum had battled with what Dad humorously called his 'ablutions'.

Anything that meant Gordon had to interact with soap and water had been a real problem. He hated having his hair shampooed, soap on his body and, worst of all, a toothbrush and toothpaste in his mouth. The smell of most toiletries made him retch. If Gordon had his own way he would never do any of these horrid things!

Learning About Friendship

Tooth-brushing was particularly difficult. Mum, Dad and the dentist had tried to persuade Gordon of the need for regular brushing, flossing and mouth-washing. However, it was not until he got a painful toothache that Gordon reluctantly agreed to brush his teeth twice a day, for at least three minutes each time. He tried to get away with just thirty seconds, but Mum would be on tooth patrol and find him out. He would then have to lie on the bed with his mouth open wide whilst Mum went in with the toothbrush to give his teeth a 'thorough clean'.

Now that Gordon was seven years old, Mum thought he was getting a bit too big for this – so now he had a 'hygiene schedule' he was supposed to follow, if he wanted any pocket money each week.

Clean clothes were another problem area. Gordon hated the smell and feel of freshly laundered clothes next to his skin. He would try to hide his favourite jeans and T-shirts from Mum, in the hope that they would escape the washing machine. However, as soon as he left for school, Mum would rummage through his things and sniff out any 'dirty' items.

Gordon could not wait until he was old enough to have his own place to live. He often said he would never bathe, brush his teeth or wash his clothes, ever again!

Learning About Friendship

Now that the hot weather was here, Mum had told Gordon he must do his 'ablutions' properly. However, since Mum had started a new job, Gordon could often get away with the minimum of washing – at least until the weekend. Then Mum would insist on standing over him whilst he completed everything on his schedule.

Ablutions

One hot summer's day at school, Mrs Goodwin, Gordon's class teacher, sent him along to the nurse's office. Gordon had no idea why, he didn't feel ill or anything.

Gordon knocked on the nurse's door.

"Enter!" bellowed Nurse Jaggard.

Gordon pushed open the door and went into the room.

Nurse Jaggard got up to open a window.

"Sit down, Gordon," said Nurse Jaggard as she pointed towards the chair by the open window.

"Gordon, we need to have a serious talk," Nurse Jaggard began. "I have had several complaints from your classmates. It seems Gordon – and there is no kind way to put this – it seems you smell, rather badly."

Learning About Friendship

Much to the nurse's surprise, Gordon did not seem at all embarrassed about being told he smelled.

"Oh well, now they know how I feel," he answered, bluntly. "Mrs Goodwin's perfume is gross and the smell of cooking from the canteen makes me feel ill," continued Gordon, screwing up his face in disgust.

"Well, that is as it may be Gordon; but most people don't usually find those sorts of smells bad. You have something called B.O. That stands for 'body odour'. In this hot weather you need to be extra careful about washing," Nurse Jaggard explained, matter of factly.

Ablutions

"Sheesh! Here we go again – ablutions," thought Gordon crossly.

"Do you know about keeping yourself clean, Gordon?" the nurse asked, searchingly.

"I sure do," answered Gordon, "I just don't like doing it. Why should I anyway?" he asked, cheekily.

"Well, apart from keeping you healthy, you need to think about others," Nurse Jaggard answered sharply.

Gordon was confused; why should he need to think about others? It just did not make sense.

Learning About Friendship

Seeing the puzzled look on Gordon's face, the nurse thought of a plan.

"I can see you don't quite understand, Gordon," said the nurse more kindly. "Here is what I want you to do. Today is Tuesday, for the rest of this week I want you to be a people-watcher. A sort of undercover detective."

Gordon could relate to this, one of his special interests was Inspector Gadget. He listened very carefully.

"I want you to write down the things your classmates do when you sit near them, line up with them or do group work with them. Report to me on Monday morning at 0900 hours, sharp!" Nurse Jaggard commanded as she ushered him towards the door.

Ablutions

Gordon was a bit confused, but he liked the idea of being an undercover detective and he decided he would begin as soon as he got back to class.

As he entered the classroom he noticed Melissa Fisher, a pretty, blonde girl, hold her nose and wrinkle up her face in what looked like disgust.

Gordon went straight to his workstation and wrote this down.

Then Michael Miller put his hand up.

"Please Mrs Goodwin, can I open some more windows, it stinks in here!" he complained as he got up from his chair. Some of the children sniggered behind their hands as they looked at Gordon.

Gordon noticed this and wrote it down in his 'detective book'.

Learning About Friendship

"Right class, it is time for assembly. Line up at the door, please," instructed Mrs Goodwin, sternly.

The children lined up and it was then that Gordon noticed no one wanted to stand in front of or behind him. Michael Miller was pushing Gerry Mitchell towards him. Mrs Goodwin got very cross with them and made them go to the back of the line.

"RESULT!" cheered Michael, cheekily, as he and Gerry moved down the line.

Ablutions

Gordon did not need to wait until Monday morning to see Nurse Jaggard. Being a people watcher had taught him something all those years of his Mum's nagging had failed to do. If you wanted to be popular and have friends, you'd better not smell bad! As soon as Gordon realized he was doing his ablutions for other people, not just for himself, he was a changed boy.

On Wednesday morning Gordon got his first real compliment. It was from Mrs Goodwin.

"Goodness me, Gordon, don't you look nice," she enthused as she saw his shiny hair and smart, clean clothes.

"Thank you, Mrs Goodwin," replied Gordon with a shy smile.

Then Melissa Fisher asked him if he would like to be in her group for history next lesson.

Learning About Friendship

Gordon felt really happy. He still hated ablutions, but now when he did them, he thought about how friendly his classmates had become. Even his dad noticed the change in him and he got a rise in pocket money.

These days Mum does not have to watch over Gordon's daily ablutions; he has got himself into a neat little routine. It does not take too long and he has been getting quite a lot of attention from the girls in his class. You see, they had never realized how handsome Gordon was, until they saw him in clean clothes with shining hair and a gleaming, white smile! In fact all the kids in his class are more friendly – even Michael Miller!

Story 7

Space Invaders

A Story About Personal Space

Overview

Personal space is that often variable, invisible area around our body that we regard as belonging to us, exclusively. If someone encroaches on this space we may feel anxious or angry. Studies have shown that it is that part of the brain (already implicated in ASD), called the 'amygdala', which is activated when people get too close physically. Quite often children with ASD are either *hyper*sensitive to people standing too close and try to avoid this, or *hypo*sensitive and actively seek out physical contact, not always appropriately.

I have witnessed both types of child in the mainstream classroom. There is the child who simply has to be at the front or back of every queue, or, preferably, allowed to leave first or last in order to avoid a queue. Then there is the child who loves to line up, getting as close as possible to the child in front and often causing havoc as the teacher strives to arrange the class in an orderly line for transitions.

Learning about personal space is an important social rule. Most NT children know instinctively when they enter someone's personal space and when someone enters theirs. However, children with ASD – and, indeed, other special needs – require teaching to help them to recognize and respond to these invisible boundaries. Children who constantly invade personal space, although endearing when very young, can soon be seen as threatening or just odd. Strangely, they are often totally unaware of the way they make other children feel. This will, inevitably, lead to a difficulty making friends and their being rejected by peers, especially as they move from pre-school to main school. An inability to process personal-space boundaries may also mean these children could be vulnerable to inappropriate conduct from adults, and so it is an essential life skill.

In the story 'Space Invaders', we see how a young, newly qualified teacher tackles the issue of personal-space violations. After reading and discussing the story, the child could be taken on a 'personal-space journey' to enable him or her to observe first hand the way proximity changes in different settings. Learning 'elevator etiquette' (for example people usually all face in the same direction in an elevator) is a good place to start. Practise joining a queue at the post office, bank and supermarket. Take a ride on a crowded bus or tube train. Negotiate your way to seats in a crowded cinema. All of these need to be taught explicitly so the child becomes mindful of personal-space boundaries.

It is often better to exaggerate personal-space boundaries with young children and children with ASD, as this will make this abstract concept more tangible. There are many children with ASD who feel extremely threatened when their personal space is invaded. It can lead to misunderstandings during transition times, in the dinner queue or out in the school playground. By ensuring other children are aware of this issue and therefore mindful of the needs of the child with ASD, it can help to prevent these potential hot spots from bubbling over into bad behaviour.

Space Invaders

Miss Preston was feeling very tired. Her Class 2 children had just gone home and she made her way to the staff room for a well-earned cup of tea.

"I don't know," she said wearily, as she sank into a comfy armchair. "My class are really lovely, but they can't seem to line up properly, and just recently Emily Lucas has been trying to sit on my knee during circle time. Now other children are clamouring to get on too – I'm quite exhausted!"

"Oh dear," commented Miss Rutland, the Deputy Head Teacher, "it seems your class need a lesson on 'personal space."

"Personal space?" enquired Miss Preston with interest.

Learning About Friendship

"Yes, my dear," continued Miss Rutland, "personal space! Some children just don't know about keeping the right distance from others. They squash up together when lining up and some children get far too close to the teacher. It happened to me when I was newly qualified. Then one day, my headmistress told me how to cure the problem."

Miss Preston sat up in her chair and listened intently whilst Miss Rutland told her what to do.

The next day as the children entered the classroom they were met by a very amusing sight. Miss Preston was sporting a huge, inflatable rubber ring around her slender waist. On the floor in front of her chair were strewn a number of hula-hoops, one for each child.

"Come in Class 2," greeted Miss Preston, cheerfully. "Find a hoop and sit in it, please."

The children raced to the hoops and sat cross-legged in front of Miss Preston, grinning from ear to ear.

Space Invaders

"Well done, children," she said encouragingly, "a very good morning to you all. I suppose you are wondering why you are sitting in hoops and why I am wearing this rubber ring."

"Yes, Miss Preston," the children chanted, eyes gleaming.

"Well, today we are going to learn about 'personal space'. We all have an invisible bubble around our bodies that we call our 'personal space'. 'Invisible' means we can't see it, but it is there!" stressed Miss Preston.

The children were enthralled.

"Emily Lucas," continued Miss Preston, "stand up please. Now Emily, I would like you to stretch out your arms and turn slowly in a circle. Are you all watching Emily? Emily is showing you where her personal space is. Thank you, Emily, sit down dear."

Emily sat down and smiled broadly, she loved to help out Miss Preston.

Learning About Friendship

"Now, children," Miss Preston said in a stern voice, but with a twinkle in her eyes, "I have noticed that some of you are becoming 'Space Invaders!' You get too close to each other *and* to me. When someone meets a space invader it can make us feel very uncomfortable, angry or even afraid."

Nigel Slater put his hand up.

"Yes, Nigel," enquired Miss Preston.

"I feel strange when people get too close to me," said Nigel, earnestly, "that's why I like to stay on the end of the line."

"Thank you, Nigel," continued Miss Preston. "I did notice that. We should try our best not to get too close to the other people in the line. They may be like Nigel and feel uncomfortable. We don't want to burst their personal space bubbles, do we?" she said with a smile.

Miss Preston leaned forward in her chair.

Space Invaders

"The size of your personal space bubble will change depending on who you are with," went on the teacher.

She reached into a box and brought out a piece of rope. She fashioned the rope into a small circle on the floor.

"Nigel, would you come and sit inside the rope, please," she asked, kindly.

Nigel got up and facing the class he sat cross-legged in the rope.

"Now, imagine this rope shows where Nigel's personal space is. It is quite small here; this shows Nigel's personal space when he is at home with his family. At home, your personal space may be very small, we all enjoy getting close to people we love and know very well. However, at school Nigel's personal space bubble is much bigger," she explained, adjusting the rope to make a bigger circle.

"Now put your hand up if you can think when Nigel's personal space bubble may get even bigger," enquired Miss Preston.

Learning About Friendship

Andy Gilbert, the class clown, put his hand up in an instant. "Near someone who smells bad, Miss," he answered, cheekily.

"Well, Andy, I think you know that is not really the sensible answer I was looking for. Try again, Andy, please," said Miss Preston, patiently.

Andy went red, but thought very hard. "Strangers, Miss, people we don't know and we shouldn't get close to," he answered, earnestly.

"Andy Gilbert, you are a star! Kindly put three marbles in the class jar," said Miss Preston, enthusiastically.

Andy beamed, all the children knew that when the jar was full they were going to watch a Disney movie and have popcorn, just like in the cinema.

Miss Preston smiled, the lesson was going well and the children seemed very interested. She could not remember the last time she got a sensible response from Andy Gilbert.

Space Invaders

"Sometimes,' continued Miss Preston, "there are times when we have to invade personal space because we don't have a choice. Can anyone think of an example?"

The children looked at each other and thought hard. Amy Smith put her hand up slowly.

"Yes, Amy?" enquired the teacher.

"Er, is it like in a busy lift or on a bus or tube train?" asked Amy, tentatively.

"Super answer, Amy. Two marbles in the jar, please," said Miss Preston, with a wink.

"Amy was exactly right, if we don't have a choice because the place is crowded, then it is okay to go into someone's personal space, but we should still do our best not to touch them. If we touch accidentally, we should always smile and say 'sorry'," explained the teacher.

"Now children, we are going into the playground to play a game. Keeping inside your hoops, line up by the door sensibly, thinking about personal space," she reminded the children.

There was a lot of crashing of hoops as the children went to line up, but after just two minutes the class had lined up beautifully with just the right amount of space between them.

Out in the playground Miss Preston told the children that they were going to play a game. She would be a 'Space Invader' and they would play 'Space Chase'. In this game she would try to touch the children's hoops, and if she succeeded it meant she had burst their personal space bubble and they should sit on the ground inside the hoops, as they would be 'out'.

The children ran about excitedly, but it was not long before everyone was seated on the ground. Miss Preston had managed to touch everyone's hoops.

"Well done, children," said Miss Preston, breathlessly, "now line up, still in your hoops, and we will go back inside for a story."

Miss Preston was very impressed with the way the children lined up and sat down on the carpet again.

As all the children were seated quietly, Miss Preston got out the big book for story time. Emily Lucas left her place on the floor and tried to get up onto Miss Preston's knee. However, the rubber ring around the teacher's waist made it very difficult for her to get on.

"Now, Emily, can you see that when you try to sit on my knee you are being a personal space invader?" Miss Preston pointed out kindly.

Space Invaders

Emily nodded, but she was confused. She knew Miss Preston very well and she loved her, so why couldn't she sit on her knee?
"But I love you, Miss Preston," pleaded Emily.

"I know, dear; but I am your teacher, not your mummy. I have many children in my class. Suppose they all wanted to sit on my knee – I would be very, very tired by the end of the school day," she explained.

Emily went back to her place on the carpet. She would have liked to sit on the teacher's knee, as she did in pre-school, but she did not want to be a space invader.

Miss Preston made a special story for Emily all about personal space. She gave it to her to read at home, and Emily snuggled up close to Mummy that night, as they read the story together.

You will be pleased to know that all the children in Miss Preston's class remembered the lesson on personal space and before long they were enjoying a Disney film and popcorn!

Story 8

Billy Blunt

A Story About Using Tact and Diplomacy

Overview

There will not be many families, or people who know and work with children with autism, that cannot relate to this story. We may all have a bank of embarrassing moments that have happened over the years due to such a child's brutal frankness. However, we do not always take the time to consider these moments from the perspective of the young person with ASD. They, too, will have to endure disapproving glances and chastisement from family, friends, teachers and, sometimes, strangers. However, unlike us NT folk, they may genuinely be surprised and confused at the reactions some of their guileless comments may produce.

Children with autism are often described as being 'blunt', 'to the point' or 'brutally honest', and are judged accordingly. We forget that this disorder means that they:

- cannot feign interest if they do not feel it
- do not aspire to gain social approval by means of flattery
- fail to understand the need to tell 'little white lies' to avoid hurting someone's feelings, and
- lack the social nous to know when some questions are inappropriate.

Children on the autism spectrum have the desire to interact socially, but they need to be taught, in a direct way, those social skills that other children pick up intuitively using their powers of observation.

Learning About Friendship

In the story, Billy Blunt is forever getting into trouble for saying the wrong thing. At heart, he is a caring, sympathetic individual with a desire to please, but his lack of pretence, child-like curiosity and impulsivity lead to his being constantly in trouble and failing to make and maintain friends.

Whilst we may smile at some of his antics, it very soon becomes clear that unless Billy changes his ways he will not be able to form good relationships with his peers. The teacher in this story uses a technique called 'cartoon-strip conversations' devised by Carol Gray (see the Appendix for details), to enable Billy to see the results of his impulsive comments and impertinent questions. The knowledge gained by Billy from this process helps him to think before speaking and thus save himself, and others, from embarrassing *faux pas* and hurt feelings.

As you read this story, get the child to explore the feelings of the other characters:

- Why was Billy's sister upset?
- Why did Great Aunt Winifred go home early?
- Why did Simon's face go red?

It is only by capturing the moment and getting the child to view it from all sides that they will grow in social knowledge and understanding.

Billy Blunt

Billy Blunt was blunt by name and blunt by nature. Billy just did not know why, but he often got into trouble for saying something that seemed perfectly okay to him. Why, just the other day, when old Mrs Bleasdale had called in for tea, he was sent to his room for mentioning the fact that she had a long hair growing from her chin. The hair had fascinated Billy. It must have been over one centimetre long and he wondered if anyone could grow one. Surely it was not wrong to ask Mrs Bleasdale how long she had been growing it? However, his mum, choking on her buttered teacake, had sent him to his room.

Learning About Friendship

Then there was the time that his older sister, Barbara, had been getting ready to go to a disco with a new boy from her class. It had taken her rather a long time to get ready and when she heard the doorbell ring, she asked Billy to go downstairs and say she would be down shortly. Billy, always happy to help, had raced to the door to deliver the message. How was he to know that Barbara would become enraged when she heard him tell the boy that she would be down shortly, after she had finished shaving her hairy legs? Billy thought he was being helpful, but the boy decided not to wait and said he would see Barbara at the disco later. There had been a terrible upset, tears from Barbara and the whole thing led to Billy being sent to his room with an 'Oh, *how could you*, Billy?' from his mum.

There was another incident that Billy remembered that had resulted in Dad being very cross with him all Christmas day. Great Aunt Winifred came every year for Christmas lunch and every year Dad wondered what present they should give her. He often said, jokingly, that it was 'not easy choosing the right gift for the silly old bag.'

That Christmas they decided to give her a leather handbag that someone had given to Mum. Mum thought it a bit old-fashioned, and Dad said it would be the perfect gift for Great Aunt Winifred.

When Great Aunt Winifred opened her gift, Billy could see that she was truly delighted.

"Oh, now how did you know I needed a new bag?" she said with a smile.

"Oh, we didn't know," blurted out Billy, truthfully, "someone gave it to Mum last Christmas, but she thought it was old-fashioned and so Dad thought it would be good to give the bag to you because you are a silly old bag."

Billy had to spend the rest of Christmas day in his room and Great Aunt Winifred had gone home early that year with a 'headache'.

Learning About Friendship

One day at school, Mr Bennett, Billy's teacher, informed the class that a new boy would be joining them and they should all be super friendly to make him feel welcome. The boy's name was Simon Smedley. Mr Bennett introduced him to the class and he was given the only empty seat, right next to Billy. Billy smiled at Simon in a friendly way; he hoped they could become best buddies. All the other children seemed to have a best friend, but not Billy.

As Simon took his seat, Billy noticed a funny red mark on Simon's cheek.

"Hey, Simon," asked Billy, in a rather loud voice, "what's that on your cheek?"

Simon's face turned bright red.

"Billy Blunt, kindly leave the classroom, immediately," called out Mr Bennett, sternly.

Billy was about to ask why, but thought he had better just do as he was told.

Billy Blunt

Mr Bennett made Billy stay in at playtime to finish off the maths work he had missed when he had to leave the classroom. Billy noticed that Simon's chair had been moved to Sarah Morgan's table.

"Why am I always getting into trouble?" Billy asked Mr Bennett.

"Do you really not know?" asked the teacher, raising his eyebrows.

"I think I probably ask too many questions," continued Billy, "but it is only because I am curious."

"No, Billy, it is not because you ask too many questions, although you do; it is because you say things without thinking," explained Mr Bennett.

He could see that Billy was still confused.

"Let us have lunch together tomorrow, Billy, and I will try to explain what I mean," suggested the teacher.

Learning About Friendship

The very next day, Billy stayed in the classroom to eat his lunch with Mr Bennett.

Mr Bennett had a large piece of paper and some marker pens. "Now, Billy, I want you to imagine that this is you." He drew a stick figure with a huge speech bubble coming from its mouth. In the bubble were the words: "Hey, Simon, what's that on your cheek?"

"This is what happened yesterday. Is that right?" asked the teacher.

"Yes," answered Billy, unconcerned.

"Now let's look at the other people involved and see what they are thinking," continued Mr Bennett. He drew another stick person with a speech bubble coming from his head.

"Imagine this is Simon," he went on, "what do you think Simon is thinking?"

"He is thinking that this boy," Billy said, pointing to his own stick figure, "is really friendly. He is smiling at me and asking me a question."

Billy Blunt

"No, Billy," stressed Mr Bennett, "he most certainly is not! Simon is thinking: why is this boy trying to make fun of me by asking about my birth mark? Now all the children will be laughing at me. I am really embarrassed. I wish I were still in my old school!"

"No, no, I didn't mean to do that, I was just interested," explained Billy, fighting back the tears.

"Yes, I believe you, Billy, but others won't," Mr Bennett said, kindly. "They will think you were being mean. What do you think *I* was thinking when I sent you out of the room?" he continued.

"You were probably cross because I was talking when I should have been listening," answered Billy.

Mr Bennett drew a stick figure to show what he had been thinking. Out of the thought bubble it said: 'Oh, no, that Billy Blunt has done it again. He has hurt the new boy's feelings. How vexing when I just asked them to be super-friendly. I will have to send him out and I'll ask Sarah to sit with Simon, because she is so kind and helpful.'

Learning About Friendship

Billy was speechless with shock. How could he have upset so many people? He began to cry, and Mr Bennett told him not to worry. He would explain to the class that Billy had a little difficulty understanding how people thought. They all liked Billy and could see that he meant well. However, he urged Billy to think before he spoke in future.

Later that evening, Billy told Mum, Dad and Barbara about the cartoons Mr Bennett had drawn. They thought it was a brilliant idea. Barbara showed him why she had been upset when Billy mentioned she was shaving her legs. Dad explained why telling Great Aunt Winifred about the gift had hurt her feelings and made them all feel embarrassed. He also added that he had been wrong to jokingly call her a 'silly old bag'.

"So, you see, Billy," said Dad, "we can all make mistakes when we say something without thinking, even me!"

Billy Blunt

The next day at school Billy went up to Simon Smedley. "Hey, Simon, I am really sorry that I upset you yesterday. I did not mean to, in fact I was just trying to be friendly," said Billy, intently.

"Oh, that's all right. I was feeling nervous because everything was new. The mark on my cheek is called a 'strawberry spot'. I was born with it and it should fade a bit as I get older," explained Simon.

"Strawberries are my most favourite fruit," smiled Billy. "Would you like to come for tea at my house some time?" asked Billy, hopefully.

"I sure would, but only if we can have strawberries and cream!" added Simon with a grin.

The next day at school Billy went up to Simon Smedley. 'Hey, Simon, I am really sorry that I upset you yesterday. I did not mean it. In fact I was just trying to be friendly,' said Billy meekly.

'Oh, that's all right. I was feeling nervous because everything is so new. The mark on my cheek is called a strawberry, as I was born with it and it should fade a bit,' the boy at school explained.

'Strawberries are my most favourite fruit, smiled Billy. 'Would you like to come for tea at my house some time?' asked Billy hopefully.

'There would be my Mum and Dad, two sisters and me and Oskar Barker, our tortoise.'

Story 9

The Barbie Club

A Story About Being Taken Advantage Of

Overview

Quite often children with ASD fail to distinguish between when other children are being genuinely friendly and when they are just using them. They have no real powers of discernment. They are so anxious to fit in and place such little value on material possessions that they can become easy targets for the class bully or the less scrupulous child who stands to gain from their naivety.

Sometimes we just have to accept that some children are unkind, that more vulnerable children may fall victim to them and that other children will be too intimidated to do anything about it.

In this story I wanted to highlight a common problem – that of trying to 'buy' friends. It is not only children with ASD who are prone to this. Often parents or teachers recognize when the child with ASD is being taken advantage of, but it is very difficult to explain this to the child and often they refuse to believe what they are being told. If giving away lunch money or a favourite toy or game will get them included, then they will think this is a fair exchange.

Sometimes, being privy to another person's thoughts can be most enlightening for a child with ASD. After reading the story you can discuss why it is was wrong for Sally to ask Belinda to give her the doll. You can demonstrate that you do not always need to be part of a group, especially if it is led by a mean child.

It is much easier to make friends with just one child. In the story the teacher has the right intentions when she appoints a play buddy, but she has not followed through to see whether it was working. By talking through the story and taking each person's perspective, we can really help a child with ASD to understand how easy it is for friendships to go wrong and for people to be tricked or taken advantage of.

Learning About Friendship

The Barbie Club

It was Belinda's birthday. She had been given many presents, but her favourite was a new Barbie doll to add to her collection.

Belinda had been collecting Barbies for over two years; they were her passion, and she played with them whenever she could.

The Barbie Club

Mum had been saving up to buy her the latest in the Barbie series.

"Now, do be careful with it, darling, it cost a great deal of money," said Mum.

Learning About Friendship

Belinda took it to her bedroom and lined it up with her other Barbies. She kept all the accessories in special labelled boxes and they took pride of place in her bedroom. She enjoyed counting them and they were always lined up in the same order.

The Barbie Club

Mum had invited six girls to come around for a birthday tea party. Amongst them was Sally Stevenson. Sally lived in the next street and she was in Belinda's class at school. Sally didn't really like Belinda, but her mother had made her attend the party.

"It is just a couple of hours, darling. I see Belinda's mum everyday and it would be awkward if you don't go. *Please!* Just for me," pleaded Sally's mum.

Learning About Friendship

At the party, after cutting the Barbie doll birthday cake, Belinda's mum suggested the girls go up to Belinda's bedroom to play.

Sally's eyes nearly popped out of her head when she saw all the dolls lined up. Sally loved Barbie dolls, but since her dad had been laid off work she had not been able to afford any new ones. Sally's mum picked up some second-hand ones at the boot sales she liked to attend.

The Barbie Club

The next day at school Miss Hughes, the class teacher, asked Sally's group if they would look after Belinda at playtime. She had noticed that Belinda was often alone during recess and lunch break.

"Do we have to, Miss?" grumbled Sally.

"It would be a kind thing to do," suggested Miss Hughes.

Sally had an idea, "Well, Belinda is mad about Barbies. Could we bring one to school and have a Barbie Club?" asked Sally.

Usually Miss Hughes discouraged the children from bringing toys into school, but this seemed like a good idea.

"I think that would be okay," she agreed.

Learning About Friendship

At home later that day, Belinda was really excited.

"Miss Hughes says that we can take a Barbie to school and I am going to play with Sally and some girls in my class. We are having a Barbie Club," she said, her eyes shining.

"Oh, I don't know dear," said her mum. "They may get damaged or stolen."

"I'll be very careful," Belinda promised.

The Barbie Club

The next day at playtime Sally started the Barbie Club.

"I'm the leader, 'cos it was my idea," boasted Sally.

The girls had a really good time playing, but Sally was aware that her Barbie looked old and tired next to Belinda's new one.

"If you want to be in my Barbie Club," Sally told Belinda later, "you have to give me your new doll."

Learning About Friendship

"Oh, okay," said Sally. She desperately wanted to be in the Barbie Club, so she happily handed over the doll to Sally.

"Are you my best friend now?" Belinda asked, innocently.

"Oh, yeah, right," smirked Sally. "My very best friend," she added, sarcastically.

The Barbie Club

"Hey, that's Belinda's doll," said Mandy Jackson the next day.

"No it isn't – Belinda gave it to me, didn't you Belinda?" Sally challenged.

"Oh, yes, I did," said Belinda smiling broadly. "Sally is my very best friend."

Learning About Friendship

Later Mandy spoke to Sally.

"How did you manage to get Belinda to give you her new Barbie doll?" she asked, enviously.

"Oh, it was easy, I told her she couldn't be in our club unless she gave it to me. She is such a loser – she handed it over without question," gloated Sally.

Mandy felt uncomfortable about what Sally had said. She knew she should tell the teacher, but she did not want Sally to be mean to her, so she did nothing.

The Barbie Club

That night as Belinda got into bed, her mum noticed the new doll was missing.

"Oh, Belinda," she challenged, "you haven't forgotten your new Barbie at school, have you?"

"Oh, no," said Belinda, innocently, "I gave it to Sally, she's my best friend."

"What do you mean – you gave it to Sally? It's your brand new birthday doll!" shouted Mum, crossly.

"Well, it is my doll and I can give it to who I want," said Belinda, defiantly. "Besides, Sally said if I didn't give her the doll, I couldn't be in her Barbie Club. I love the Barbie Club," said Belinda, revealingly.

"Oh, darling, don't you know you can't buy friends. Sally was wrong to take your doll and I am going to see Miss Hughes about this tomorrow," said Mum, sternly.

Learning About Friendship

"NO! NO!" shrieked Belinda. "Don't do that, I'll be thrown out of the club and Miss Hughes will stop us bringing our dolls to school. All the girls will hate me." Belinda began to sob.

Mum could feel a meltdown coming on. This probably wasn't the best time to discuss this with her.

"Okay, calm down," pleaded Mum, "I won't speak to Miss Hughes, but I will mention it to Sally's mum. Now you go to sleep."

Belinda was relieved; she didn't want anything to spoil the Barbie Club.

The Barbie Club

The next day Belinda's mum went to see Mrs Stevenson. She explained about the Barbie doll.

"I can't believe Sally would do that," said Sally's mum, anxiously. "She knows how expensive they are. I always buy them at boot sales."

"Maybe that is why she wanted a new one," said Belinda's mum, kindly.

Later that day Sally and her mum came round to Belinda's house with the doll.

Belinda hid behind her mother and Sally's eyes were red, as if she had been crying. Belinda was really pleased to have her doll back in her collection.

Sally and her mum would not stay for tea and cake; they left as soon as they handed the doll back. Sally felt angry and humiliated. She would show that Belinda a thing or two at school tomorrow.

Learning About Friendship

The next day at recess, Belinda joined her friends at the Barbie Club, but they all turned their backs on her.

"GET LOST!" shouted Sally. "You're not in our club, we don't want you anymore."

Belinda felt hurt and confused. Her mother hadn't told the teacher, so why was everyone angry with her?

The Barbie Club

Belinda felt very sad and lonely. She went to the other side of the playground to play with her doll, but it was no fun on her own. Great tears welled up in her eyes and she felt a huge lump in her throat.

A girl called Lucy came over to her.

"Hey Belinda," she asked, quietly, "are you okay? I couldn't help but overhear Sally."

Belinda looked up, she just could not understand why Sally had excluded her from the club.

Learning About Friendship

"You know, Belinda, we could start our own Barbie Club," suggested Lucy with a smile.

"I will bring my Barbie tomorrow and we can play together. I'll even get my mum to organize a play date at my house – would you like that?" she enquired, hopefully.

"Oh, yes please," said Belinda, excitedly.

From that day on, Belinda and Lucy became the best of friends. Belinda learned that you can't make people like you by giving them things.

Friendship means so much more than that.

Story 10

The Beach Ball

A Story About Jealousy and What Makes a Friend

Overview

In this story Callum has difficulty understanding why he has not been invited to a birthday party. His perception of what a friend is like is immature and naive. The class teacher helps him to understand that friendship is a skill which needs to be nurtured if it is to grow and stand the test of time. She uses a device that works really well for children with ASD – a Mind Map*. This helps the child to develop thinking skills by making connections between information and ideas.

In this story Callum successfully uses some of the strategies the teacher suggests to make a friend. However, he then spoils everything by acting in an unkind and jealous way. This story emphasizes that life isn't easy and making friends is a skill. To attract people you have to care about them. This means listening to what they have to say. Children with ASD need to know that it is possible for people to have more than one friend and that jealousy is a sure way to drive someone away. Sometimes children with ASD can only manage to have one friend at a time.

Being part of a group holds many challenges and this could have been the real reason behind Callum's anger. Children with ASD need to learn that most people enjoy having lots of friends and that it is okay to do different activities with different people.

However, they also need to learn that tomorrow is another day and that we can always learn from our mistakes and move on.

---

* From Buzan, T. (2006) *Mind Mapping: Kick Start Your Creativity and Transform Your Life.* Harlow: BBC Active.

Learning About Friendship

The Beach Ball

Callum was crashing around in the classroom. He felt both sad and angry at the same time.

Miss Jones, Callum's class teacher, could sense something was wrong and she asked him to wait behind when all the other children went out for playtime.

The Beach Ball

"Now, Callum, I can see that something is bothering you. Please tell me. Maybe I will be able to help," Miss Jones said, kindly. Callum stared at his feet.

"It's Mark, Miss. I feel angry with him and it is making me feel sort of sad as well," explained Callum.

"Whatever has happened? Has Mark done something to hurt your feelings?" enquired Miss Jones, earnestly.

"Well, it's his birthday next Saturday and some of the kids have got an invitation to his party, but he hasn't given one to me," Callum said, sadly. He felt like he was going to cry.

Learning About Friendship

"Is Mark a particular friend of yours Callum?" asked Miss Jones. "I don't recall you doing very much with him."

"Well, he is my classmate and he is always nice to me, so I must be his friend, mustn't I?" pondered Callum, sulkily.

Miss Jones smiled sympathetically.

"Callum, I don't think you understand what a friend is. A friend isn't just someone you know, who is kind to you. A friendship is special. You need to do things to make a friendship grow," explained Miss Jones.

"Make it grow?" gasped Callum. Now he was really confused.

The Beach Ball

"What do you mean?" Callum asked.

Miss Jones walked over to the cupboard and took something out.

"Let me try to explain," said Miss Jones, patiently. "What is this Callum?" Miss Jones asked, holding up a deflated beach ball.

Callum was puzzled, "It's a beach ball, Miss," he said, snappily, thinking Miss Jones was missing the point.

Learning About Friendship

"Can we play with it?" asked Miss Jones, throwing the ball to Callum.

"No," Callum laughed, in spite of himself, "You need to put some air in it!"

"Well, friendship is like this beach ball. We need to put something into the friendship to make it grow. Just because you know someone and they are kind to you, it doesn't make them your friend," explained Miss Jones. "It is the *start* of a friendship, just like this is the beginning of a beach ball. However, if we don't put things into the friendship, it won't grow and develop. It is just like this beach ball, we need to pump it up with air to make it big and strong so we can play with it."

The Beach Ball

"What do you mean, Miss?" asked Callum, quizzically. "How do you put air in a friend?' Miss Jones laughed.

"Not air, Callum, other things, like sharing interests, being fun, paying compliments, helping – so many things go into being a friend. If you want to be a friend, you have to help a friendship to grow, *and*," stressed Miss Jones, "you have to make sure that nothing will spoil it. If you blow up this beach ball, will that be it? Will it be a good, strong ball forever?"

Callum thought hard. "No. I guess not, it will start to go down, so you have to keep pumping air into it."

"Great answer, Callum," enthused Miss Jones. "It's just the same with friendship, if you don't look after it, you might spoil it."

Learning About Friendship

"This making friends doesn't sound as easy as blowing up a beach ball," said Callum, philosophically.

"Oh, Callum," said Miss Jones, "you are so right! Making friends and keeping friends is quite a skill. Some people think it is too hard and they don't even try. You see, you can't be a true friend if you are selfish. Friendship is all about thinking about the other person, not just about yourself. But once you have a friend, or, indeed, lots of friends, it is the finest feeling in the world."

The Beach Ball

Miss Jones smiled. "It seems playtime is over already. Let's talk about this some more with the class, maybe it will help you," said Miss Jones.

During circle time, Miss Jones typed in the word 'FRIENDSHIP' on the interactive white board. She asked the class if they could think of things to do that would make a friendship grow. The children were full of ideas.

As they spoke, Miss Jones built up a Mind Map and Callum began to understand. Mind Mapping always helped Callum because he could see how ideas fitted together and it gave him time to process the words.

Learning About Friendship

By the end of the session, Callum had lots of ideas on how to make a friendship grow. Things like: sharing, helping one another, using kind words, being supportive and paying compliments. Callum had to ask about 'paying compliments', because he thought it might have something to do with money!

However, Miss Jones explained that it meant telling someone what you admired about them or what was good about them. Miss Jones printed off the Mind Map and gave it to Callum at home time. Callum thanked her and went home to think up ways that he could grow a friendship.

The Beach Ball

That night, Callum decided he would try to make John his friend. He had once lost his temper with John, but John had forgiven him and been really great about it. He would like John as a friend. At snack time the next day, Callum offered John a cookie. Callum loved chocolate chip cookies and his mum had made extra for him that day. John seemed genuinely pleased and surprised.

"Oh, yes please, Callum," he said, gratefully.

As they sat munching the cookies John asked Callum about the maths homework. Callum was brilliant at maths, but John found it really difficult. Callum had an idea.

"Would you like to come to my house tomorrow and I could show you how to work on fractions?" Callum asked, tentatively.

"That sounds brilliant," said John. "I'll ask my Mum."

Learning About Friendship

Callum gave John his phone number, and that evening John's mum rang and spoke to Callum's mum. It was arranged that the next day, after school, John would come home with Callum and stay for tea.

Then something happened that had never happened to Callum before – he actually spoke over the telephone with John. Callum was usually afraid of the phone because he didn't always understand what people were trying to say. This time it was okay and he told John he would see him at school the next day.

The Beach Ball

Callum had been so excited that he hadn't slept very well. He just couldn't wait for the end of the school day. He had made a friend and now John was actually coming to his house. Callum's mum had been equally surprised and happy; she had tried to invite children over before, but Callum just hadn't seemed interested in them.

During lunch and playtime John and Callum played together. Usually Callum just stayed in class at the computer, but today he played chess with John and they helped Miss Jones chop up cardboard for the art lesson.

Learning About Friendship

After school Callum's mum picked them up and the boys talked and laughed all the way to Callum's house.

After spending a very enjoyable afternoon together, it was time for John to go home. Callum asked him if he would like to come over on Saturday afternoon and go bowling. John said he was sorry, but he had to go to Mark's party on Saturday. Callum was confused and he felt himself getting angry.

"Well, get lost then!" he shouted at John. "Go to Mark's party if you want, just don't come round here anymore!"

Callum's mother went red in the face.

"I am going to take John home first and then I will speak to you!" she said, sharply.

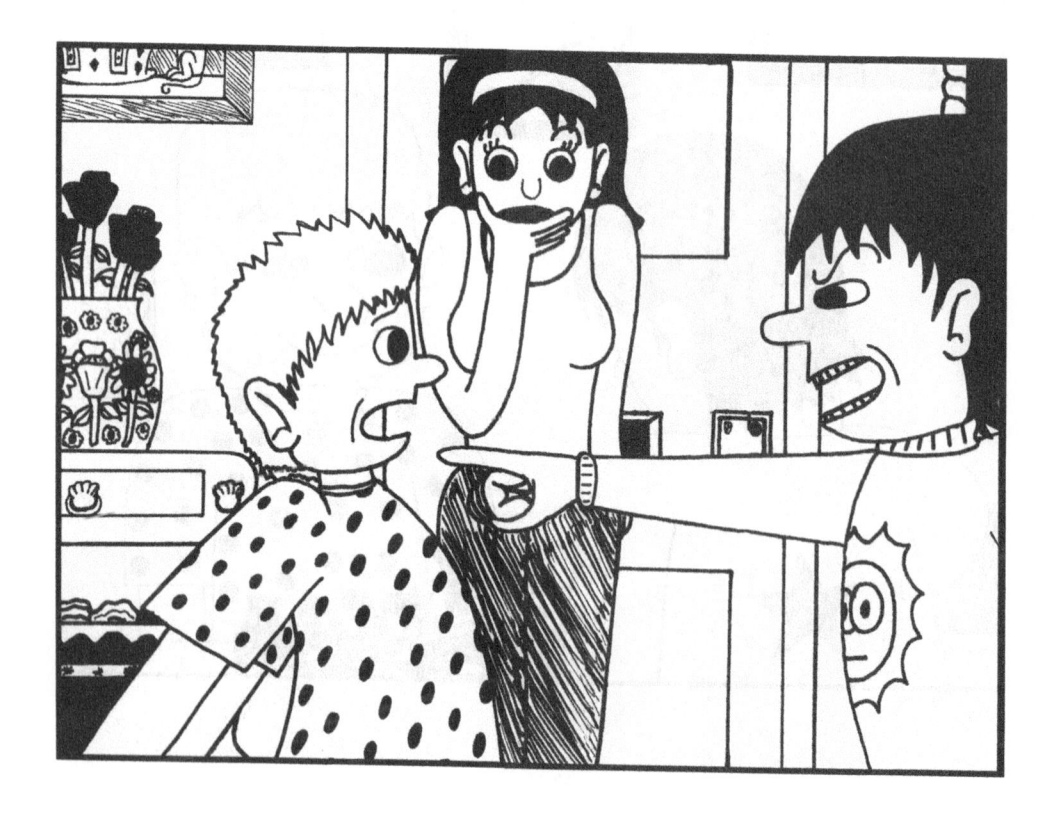

The Beach Ball

In the car, Callum's mum apologized to John.

"I am so sorry, John. You have probably noticed that knowing how to behave with a friend is something that Callum finds difficult. He didn't mean what he said."

"That's okay, maybe when Callum calms down, you could ask him if he would like to come to my house on Sunday," said John, sympathetically.

Learning About Friendship

When Callum's mum got back home, she found Callum at the computer.

"That wasn't a very friendly thing to do Callum, was it?" she challenged.

"No," said Callum warily, "I guess I've just popped the beach ball!"

"Whatever do you mean?" asked Callum's mum, curiously.

Callum explained the things Miss Jones had told him about friendship being like a beach ball, and he showed her the Mind Map.

"Well. I guess you need to do another Mind Map, pointing out all the things that can spoil a friendship," said his mum, gently.

"You feel jealous of John because he has been asked to Mark's party and you haven't, isn't that right?" asked Callum's mum, gently.

The Beach Ball

"I guess so," said Callum, sadly.

Callum and his mum sat down at the computer and made another Mind Map on ways to spoil a friendship. Jealousy, unkind words, shouting, gossiping and fighting all featured on that Mind Map.

Callum was right when he said making friends wasn't easy, but now that he knew what to do, it would get easier and easier!

Appendix: Useful Books and Resources

Books

Al-Ghani, K.I. (2008) *The Red Beast: Controlling Anger in Children with Asperger's Syndrome.* London: Jessica Kingsley Publishers.

Arnold, E. and Howley, M. (2005) *Revealing the Hidden Social Code: Social Stories for People with Autistic Spectrum Disorders.* London: Jessica Kingsley Publishers.

Baker, J. (2001) *The Social Skills Picture Book: Teaching Communication, Play and Emotion.* Arlington, Texas: Future Horizons, Inc.

Baker, J. (2003) *Social Skills Training for Children and Adolescents with Asperger Syndrome and Social-Communication Problems. Social Skills Pictures* (a series of books). Shawnee Mission, Kansas: Austism Asperger Publishing Company.

Buzan, T. (2002) *How to Mind Map.* London: Thorsons.

Buzan, T. (2006) *Mind Mapping: Kick Start Your Creativity and Transform Your Life.* Harlow: BBC Active.

Csoti, M. (2001) *Social Awareness Skills for Children.* London: Jessica Kingsley Publishers.

Day, P. (2009) *What is Friendship? Games and Activities to Help Children to Understand Friendship.* London: Jessica Kingsley Publishers.

Gray, C. (1994) *Comic Strip Conversations.* Arlington, Texas: Future Horizons Inc.

Gray, C. (2002) *My Social Stories Book.* London: Jessica Kingsley Publishers.

Gray, C. (2010) *The New Social Story Book.* Arlington, Texas: Future Horizons Inc.

Howlin, P., Baron-Cohen, S. and Hadwin, J.A. (1999) *Teaching Children with Autism to Mind-Read: A Practical Guide for Teachers and Parents.* London: J. Wiley & Sons.

Knott, F. and Dunlop, A.-W. (2007) *Developing Social Interaction and Understanding.* London: The National Autistic Society.

McAfee, J. (2001) *Navigating the Social World.* Arlington, Texas: Future Horizons Inc.

MacKay, G. and Anderson, C. (2000) *Teaching Children with Pragmatic Difficulties of Communication: Classroom Approaches.* London: David Fulton Publishers.

Myles, B.S., Trautman, M.L. and Schelvan, R.L. (2004) *The Hidden Curriculum: Practical Solutions for Understanding Unstated Rules in Social Situations.* Shawnee Mission, Kansas: Autism Asperger Publishing Company.

Patrick N.J. (2008) *Social Skills for Teenagers and Adults with Asperger's Syndrome: A Practical Guide to Day-to-Day Life.* London: Jessica Kingsley Publishers.

Pease, A. and Pease, B. (2005) *The Definitive Book of Body Language: How to Read Others' Attitudes by Their Gestures* (new edition). London: Orion Publishers.

Rinaldi, W. (1995) *The Social Use of Language Programmes.* Windsor: NFER Nelson.

Winner, M.G. (2002) *Inside Out: What Makes the Person with Social-Cognitive Deficits Tick?* London: Jessica Kingsley Publishers.

Other resources

Conversation Cubes: www.superstickers.com

Model Me Kids®: www.modelmekids.com

Pragmatic Problems Cubes: www.superstickers.com

Winslow: www.winslow-cat.com